D0605236

Makey Makey

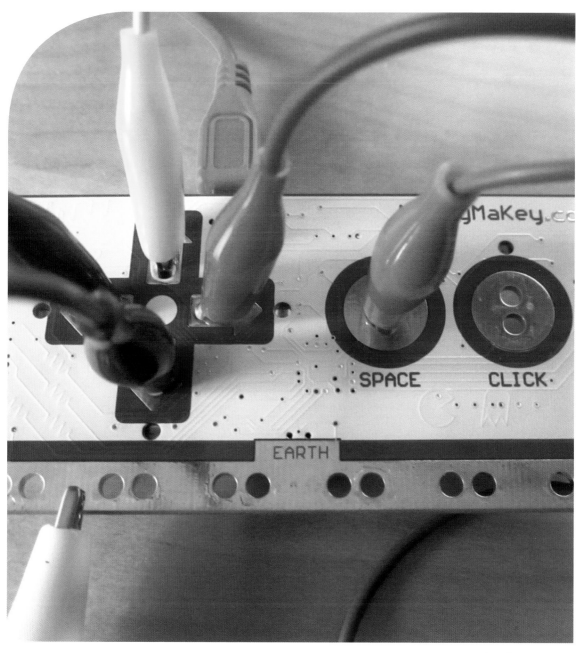

CHERRY LAKE PUBLISHING • ANN ARBOR, MICHIGAN

by Sandy Ng

A Note to Adults: Please review the instructions for the activities in this book before allowing children to do them. Be sure to help them with any activities you do not think they can safely complete on their own.

A Note to Kids: Be sure to ask an adult for help with these activities when you need it. Always put your safety first!

Published in the United States of America by Cherry Lake Publishing
Ann Arbor, Michigan
www.cherrylakepublishing.com

Series Editor: Kristin Fontichiaro
Photo Credits: Cover and page 1, Danny Nicholson / tinyurl.com/zw8fn7e /
CC BY-ND 2.0; pages 4, 7, 8, 11, 13, 16, 19, 20, 23, 24, 25, and 28,
Sandy Ng; pages 14 and 15, Amber Lovett

Library of Congress Cataloging-in-Publication Data
Names: Ng, Sandy, 1991- author.
Title: Makey Makey / by Sandy Ng.
Other titles: 21st century skills innovation library. Makers as innovators.
Description: Ann Arbor, Michigan : Cherry Lake Publishing, [2016] |
   Series: 21st Century Skills Innovation Library. Makers as innovators |
   Audience: Grades 4 to 6.- | Includes bibliographical references and index.
Identifiers: LCCN 2016000453| ISBN 9781634714143 (lib. bdg.)
 | ISBN 9781634714303 (pbk.) | ISBN 9781634714228 (pdf)
| ISBN 9781634714389 (ebook)
Subjects: LCSH: Microcontrollers—Juvenile literature. |
   Electronic circuits—Juvenile literature. | Inventions—Juvenile literature.
Classification: LCC TJ223.P76 N4 2016 | DDC 006.2/2—dc23
LC record available at http://lccn.loc.gov/2016000453

Cherry Lake Publishing would like to acknowledge the work of The Partnership for
21st Century Learning. Please visit www.p21.org for more information.

Printed in the United States of America
Corporate Graphics
July 2016

Contents

Chapter 1

Say Hello to Makey Makey

magine there's a new game you can't wait to play on your computer. You're excited to sit down and start playing. You load the game and get your fingers in position on the keyboard. However, you quickly notice that the keyboard isn't working.

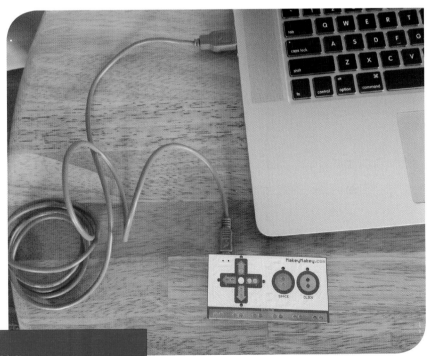

You can connect a Makey Makey to your computer and use it to control your keyboard.

To fix it, you try unplugging it and plugging it back in. It still doesn't work! How will you play your game now? Wouldn't it be great if you could just use the stuff in the room around you to build a new controller? Believe it or not, this is totally possible. You just need help from a device called a Makey Makey.

Makey Makey was created by Jay Silver and Eric Rosenbaum when they were students at the Massachusetts Institute of Technology. Jay and Eric believe that everyone in the world is creative and imaginative enough to become an inventor. They thought the only thing most people needed was an easy way to bring their ideas to life. To help these people become inventors, Jay and Eric created a simple kit called a Makey Makey.

At first, it was expensive to make the Makey Makey kits. Jay and Eric were only able to make a few of them. They needed money to make more kits so others could buy them and start inventing. In 2012, they used a Web site called Kickstarter to collect donations. Eventually, they gathered enough money and made many more kits. You can now buy either an original Makey Makey or a keychain-sized Makey Makey GO to tinker with.

All About Makers

When they were working on Makey Makey, Jay and Eric were inspired by makers. Makers are people who tinker and make things with their hands. That means you're a maker, too! Makers can be people of all ages, from 4 to 94 and beyond. They are all about trying new things. They use tools such as art supplies, sewing machines, computers, wires, and more to make their creations. Most of all, makers love to explore and use materials (such as blocks of wood, an old T-shirt, or scraps of paper) in unique and unexpected ways. As Jay once said, "I don't care that pencils are supposed to be used for writing. I'm going to use them a different way."

What Is Makey Makey?

Makey Makey comes in two versions: Classic and GO. Classic is about the size of a business card. GO can fit on a keychain and is the little sister of Classic. In this book, we'll be focusing on the Classic version. Both versions do the same thing: They help you turn everyday objects into touchpads that control your computer's keyboard. To do this, it relies on a small **circuit** board. This small but mighty circuit board works as a microcontroller. A microcontroller is a tiny computer that tells your main computer that you'd like to use other objects to control your keyboard. You can't plug a potato directly into your computer and use it to control the computer. But you could attach the potato to a Makey Makey circuit board and attach the board to the computer. If you do this, there's a good chance you could control the computer using the potato!

The microcontroller doesn't let just any object control the computer. Instead, it gives objects that can **conduct** electricity the ability to operate the computer's keyboard. We'll dive deeper into what this means later in the book.

The Makey Makey microcontroller has a simple layout that is easy to use.

With Makey Makey, you can get creative about what you want the keyboard to do. You can also choose which objects you want to use in place of keyboard keys. The Internet is full of premade programs that work with Makey Makey. They allow you to make everything from game controllers to musical instruments to light shows.

What's in the Kit?

Purchasing a classic Makey Makey kit will provide you with almost everything you need to start creating new

A Makey Makey kit comes with plenty of wires you can use in your projects.

and exciting projects. Let's open up a Makey Makey kit and take a look at everything that comes in the package. In your kit, you will find:

1 Makey Makey board: Turn the board over in your hands. You should notice that it has tiny holes and words printed on both sides. Each side works a little differently. Later on, we'll explore just what each side does. For now, we'll be using the simpler side with big arrow signs and two circles.

7 wires with alligator clips at both ends: Alligator clips are strong metal pinchers. They are used to connect the Makey Makey board to items that will later become your controllers.

6 wires without clips: You can use these wires to add more elements to your circuit or to extend the reach of the wires with alligator clips.

1 USB cable: This cable connects the board to your computer. The board can send commands and control parts of the computer through this cable. Your computer will also send power to your Makey Makey through this cable.

If you run out of wires or alligator clips, you can buy more at an electronics or hardware store. Tell someone working there that you're looking for solid core wire. Before you use this wire, get an adult to help you strip the plastic off the ends. This exposes the metal insides of the wire. You can then attach alligator clips to the exposed wire and continue your Makey Makey projects.

How Does Makey Makey Work?

All human bodies naturally produce electricity. Makey Makey acts as a connector between your body's natural electricity and the computer, creating a circuit. Who knew you could use your own human energy to control your computer?

So how does this happen? It all starts with the Makey Makey board. You've probably noticed that it has two sides. One side is pretty simple. It has four arrows marked on the board: up, down, left, and right. It also has two circles marked on the board. They are labeled "space" and "click." These arrows and circles represent keys on your keyboard. They are your **inputs**. When objects are connected to these inputs on your circuit board, they can be used to set an electrical circuit in motion.

Notice how two holes are placed on each of the inputs. You will connect alligator clips to the board using these holes. One half of the clip goes into one hole on an input. The other half goes into the other hole. If you look just below the inputs along the bottom of the board, you'll see the Earth bar. This section also has pairs of holes for attaching alligator clips. The Earth bar is important because it is a return path for electricity to come back to the board and continue

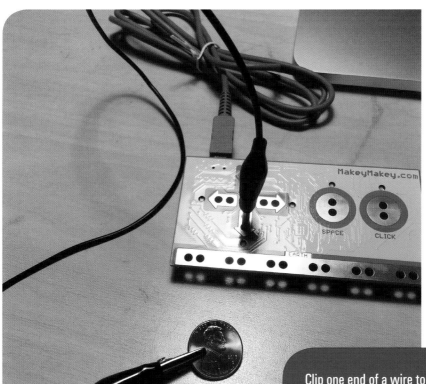

Clip one end of a wire to a penny and the other end to the down arrow holes on your circuit board.

in a circuit again. Let's test it out by using a penny to control your computer.

First, use the orange USB cable to connect the computer to the Makey Makey. Then open your Web browser and go to a site that has a lot of words and pictures on the screen, such as YouTube. Next, grab one of the wires with alligator clips at each end. Clip one of the alligator clips onto the down-arrow input of the board. Make sure it is pinching the pair of holes on the arrow. Clip the other end of the wire to the penny. This penny will serve as the keyboard's new down-arrow key.

Grab another wire with alligator clips on each end. Clip one end onto a pair of holes on the Earth bar. Use your fingertips to hold on to the clip on the wire's other end. Be careful not to pinch yourself! Use your free hand to quickly tap the penny a couple of times. Did you notice anything change on the Web site? The page moved down every time you tapped the penny. Congratulations! You just turned a penny into a down-arrow computer key. This is just one example of how you can make computer keys out of the objects

The page on your computer screen should scroll down when you tap the penny.

around you. We'll explore more things you can do with this kit later in the book.

You might be wondering why you were holding on to the metal part of an alligator clip. The answer is that you are part of the circuit that powers Makey Makey. Without you, Makey Makey won't work. Why is that? To better understand why you are an important part of this system, we first need to think about how circuits work.

Chapter 2

How Do Circuits Work?

An electrical circuit is a pathway made of wires or other conductive materials. Conductive materials are things that electricity can flow through. Examples of conductive materials include metal coins, water, and even your body. The word circuit sounds like "circle," doesn't it? There's a reason behind that. A

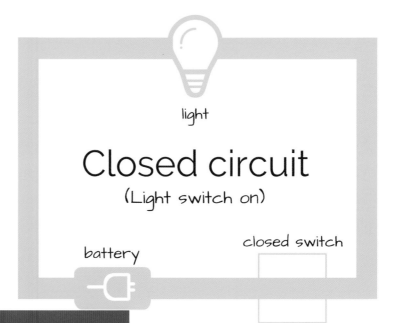

light

Closed circuit
(Light switch on)

closed switch

battery

A circuit is a complete path that electricity can travel through over and over.

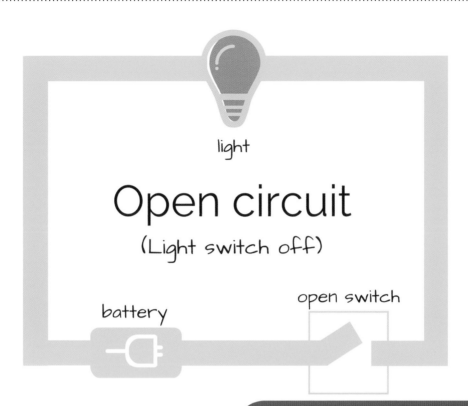

light

Open circuit
(Light switch off)

open switch

battery

In this diagram, the switch is open, breaking the circuit, so the bulb is not lit.

circuit needs to be a "circle" in order to work properly. This means that electricity needs to flow from a power source, through some wires, through a device, and back to the power source to repeat this cycle again.

Most circuits have a **switch** so they can be turned on and off. When the switch is off, it makes a gap in the circuit. This prevents the electricity from flowing through the circuit. This turns off your device. When the switch is turned on, it closes the gap. The electricity

Your body completes a circuit between an object, the Makey Makey board, a computer, and wires.

can now move through the circuit, making your device work. Every time you flip on a light switch, you're creating a circuit.

Let's take a look at the device you made earlier with the Makey Makey. Can you see how it represents a circuit? Which part is the energy source? Which parts allow electricity to flow through the circuit? Which part is the switch?

To understand the answer, you need to know about another conductive material: your body. You've probably heard that if you see a wire or power line on the ground, you should stay far away from it. You've probably also seen cartoons where someone gets electrocuted from touching a frayed wire that's plugged into a wall. The reason this happens is that our bodies conduct electricity. Power lines and electrical outlets contain a dangerous and harmful amount of electricity. But the amount of electricity used in a Makey Makey is very small. This means it can travel safely through your body. Don't try touching other electrified wires or plugs at home, though. The warning tags on lamps and appliances are there for a reason—to keep you safe!

Let's see how your conductive body works in the circuit we created in chapter one. Power flows from the computer into the Makey Makey board. Then a small amount of electricity flows from the board into the penny. Next, the electricity flows from the penny through your body. Finally, the electricity travels through your body to the alligator clip and returns to the board and computer, where it can repeat the circuit all over again.

By holding one end of the alligator clip and touching the key, your body completes the circuit. Now that the circuit is complete, Makey Makey can function. When you stop touching the key or the alligator clip, you break the circuit. Like a flipping a switch, electricity is no longer able to flow through the circuit, and the board doesn't receive a command from the key telling it to scroll down the Web page.

What Makes a Good Conductor?

Materials that allow electricity to move through them easily are called conductors. The most common type we see is a metal conductor. You've probably seen many of these around your house. They include metal prongs at the end of a plug, the metal ends of batteries, and even the thin strands of wire within a cord. We see metals in every electronic device because they are very good at conducting electricity.

Water also makes a good conductor. This is what makes your body such a good conductor. The human body is almost 60 percent water! This is also why hair dryers come with safety tags warning you not to use them near bathtubs. Dropping an electrical device into a bathtub could create a dangerous amount of electricity very quickly.

Good conductors	Poor conductors	Experiment and find out!
aluminum foil	glass	fruits
graphite (also known as pencil lead)	plastic	play dough
steel	cloth	wet sponge
brass	dry paper	household plants and flowers
copper	Styrofoam	bar of soap
water	cardboard	slice of pizza
	wood	

Chapter 3

Pianos and Potatoes

You may have played a piano before. These instruments are often big, black and white, and kind of fancy-looking. They also cost thousands of dollars. But have you ever seen a potato piano? With your Makey Makey kit, you can take everyday objects (like potatoes) and convert them into piano keys. Potatoes are both delicious and musical!

Be sure to clip one wire onto the Earth panel of your Makey Makey board.

Once all of your potatoes are connected to the board, you are ready to make some music.

Before you start, you will need a few supplies:
- 1 Makey Makey set
- A computer with a USB port
- 5 or 6 potatoes (Size and variety do not matter. Just use whatever your family has around the house.)

First, use the orange USB cable to plug your board into a USB port in your computer. Next, close any pop-up windows that appear on your computer screen. Your computer might think that your Makey Makey is another keyboard and ask you to do further setup. You don't need to take any action beyond closing the window that pops up.

Next, clip one end of a wire onto a pair of holes on the Earth panel at the bottom of your board.

The other end of the cable can be left alone for now. Clip one end of another cable onto the pair of holes in the up arrow. Clip the other end into a potato. Be sure the tip of the clip breaks through the potato's skin. Repeat this process to connect each of the left, right, and down arrows and space circle with its own potato.

Open a Web browser on your computer and go to *http://makeymakey.com/howto.php*. Scroll about halfway down the page until you find the link that says "Piano." Click on it.

Now line up your potatoes so they are in the same order as the arrangement of arrows and piano keys on the computer screen. In other words, if the screen has a piano key marked with a left arrow on the far left side of the piano, place the potato that controls the left arrow on the left side of your potato lineup.

Pick up the end of the cable that's connected to the Earth bar. Make sure you're holding on to the metal part of the clip. If needed, you can push back some of the rubber casing around the clip to hold on to more metal. With one hand holding the Earth clip, use your other hand to tap one of your potatoes and complete the circuit. Did it sound like a piano? Try tapping another potato and see how it sounds.

Staying in Touch

If you don't want to keep holding the alligator clip, you can tape it onto your skin somewhere (the back of your hand is a good spot) and keep playing. You can use masking tape, an adhesive bandage, or first aid tape. The important thing is that the metal part of the clip stays in contact with your skin so electricity can travel through your body and keep the Makey Makey circuit going.

So, What's Happening Here?

The inputs on the Makey Makey board represent the same keys on your computer keyboard. After you connected everything and touched a potato, you sent a small electric signal to the computer. That signal told the computer that a potato now controlled that computer key. In order for the computer to receive that signal, it needed to flow from the board to the potato and back to the board again. Your body became part of the circuit, allowing the signal to travel through the potato, through your body, down the cable, into the Earth bar, and back to the board again. The Makey Makey board "read" the signal and played the piano key that the computer screen said was controlled by the up arrow. Can you believe that all of this happened in less than one second? Electricity moves really quickly!

As you tap each potato, the connected piano key will light up on your screen.

Let's explore and experiment with this piano some more. What happens when you hold on to the Earth bar cable with one hand and touch two potatoes at once with your other hand? Do you hear two piano keys at the same time? Like a real piano, this potato piano lets you play more than one key at a time. What would happen if you connected multiple inputs into a single potato? What would that sound like if you tapped that potato? You can play some pretty cool mixtures of sounds with this piano that would be hard to do with a real piano.

Chapter 4

Playing with Your Feet

H ave you ever played video games like *Guitar Hero* or *Dance Dance Revolution?* In these games, players try to hit keys at just the right moment to play a song or match a beat. In this activity, you can play a similar game using your feet. The best

You can build your own controller for a fun dancing game!

Carefully secure the aluminum foil and wires to your cardboard panels.

part is that you can make the controller using materials you already have around the house. When you're done, you can even use this giant controller to play any game that uses up, down, left, and right arrows. Let's get started!

Here are the supplies you will need:
- 1 Makey Makey kit
- Scissors

- 2 empty cereal boxes
- Aluminum foil
- 1 roll of solid core wire
- Wire strippers
- Electrical tape

Your first step is to connect the Makey Makey board to the computer using the USB cable that came with your kit. Next, close any pop-up windows that appear on your computer screen. Use scissors to cut out the front and back panels of one cereal box. These are the box's largest sides. Repeat this with the second box. You should now have four sheets of cardboard. Each sheet of cardboard should be roughly the size of a sheet of note-book paper. If they are a little bigger, that's fine, too!

Cover one side of each piece of cardboard completely with aluminum foil, wrapping the foil around the edges of the cardboard. Tape down the foil on the back side to keep it in place.

Next, get an adult to help you cut five pieces of wire. Each piece should be about 4 feet (1.2 meters) long. These wires need to be long enough to reach from your computer to the ground and have around 2 feet (0.6 m) lying on the ground. You should also strip off around 2 inches (5 centimeters) of insulation from each end of the wires. This will give you plenty of exposed wire to make contact with the aluminum foil.

Use electrical tape to secure one end of each stripped wire to the top edge of each piece of card-board. Make sure the wires are touching the foil. Clip a wire with alligator clips onto the other end of each stripped wire. Make sure the clip grabs onto the metal core of the wire. Wrapping a little bit of electrical tape around the clip will help so that the wire doesn't slip out of the pinchers. Clip the other end of the alliga-tor cable onto an arrow on the Makey Makey board. Repeat this step with the other three panels until each has been connected to one arrow on your Makey Makey board.

To keep things organized, you'll want to rearrange your foil-wrapped panels so they are positioned like the keys on your keyboard. In other words, place the panel that's connected to the left arrow on your left and place the panel that's connected to the right arrow on your right. Do the same with the panels that are connected to the up and down arrows.

Tape one end of the remaining piece of stripped wire to your skin. Then clamp one end of an alligator cable onto the other end of this wire. Wrap the clip with electrical tape so the pinchers stay on the wire.

Arrange your game panels carefully before you start to play.

Finally, clamp the other end of the alligator cable onto the Earth panel of your Makey Makey board.

On your computer, go to *http://makeymakey.com /howto.php* and scroll down the page. Click on "Flash Flash Revolution" and follow the instructions on the screen.

Ready to play? Take off your shoes and socks. They don't conduct electricity well. Instead of pressing the arrows on the keyboard, you can press the sheets of cardboard with your bare feet.

Think about games you've played in the past that were controlled using the space key or any of the arrow keys. There's a good chance you can play them using this giant controller you've built. Give it a try!

Think back to the beginning of this book. You were imagining wanting to play a game but your keyboard didn't work. Remember how cool it would have been if you could make a controller on the spot so you could play your computer game? With a Makey Makey and some conductive objects from around the house, you have the tools to make your own controller. You'd be able to play that game in no time! Your controller can be made with fruit or metal spoons. As we discovered, it can even be a big controller that you use with your feet on the ground. With Makey Makey, you get to decide how you want to control your computer keys!

What Comes Next?

By now, you've learned how to take control over your computer using everyday objects. But what else could you control with a Makey Makey? What other materials could you experiment with and turn into keys? You could even try using more than one Makey Makey at a time. A computer can handle up to three kits as long as it has enough USB ports.

If you want more control over your Makey Makey inventions, you may be ready to use the other side of the board. That side has 12 more keys you can control. It can be a little more challenging because it requires learning a little bit of **code**. However, you can find helpful tips at *https://learn.sparkfun.com/tutorials/makey-makey-advanced-guide*. You may also be ready to move from Makey Makey to an Arduino. An Arduino is a powerful microcontroller that you can program from scratch to behave like a robot, sense water or light, open doors for you, and much more! There's no limit to the number of things you can invent with a microcontroller, so get out there and start making!

Glossary

circuit (SUR-kit) an uninterrupted path along which electricity can flow

code (KOHD) instructions written in a language that can be understood by computers

conduct (kuhn-DUKT) to allow electricity to pass through

inputs (IN-puts) information or signals that are received by a device

switch (SWICH) a piece of equipment that can be used to break the path of electricity in a circuit, as well as reconnect it

Find Out More

BOOKS

O'Neill, Terence, and Josh Williams. *Arduino*. Ann Arbor, MI: Cherry Lake Publishing, 2014.

Roslund, Samantha, and Kristin Fontichiaro. *Maker Faire*. Ann Arbor, MI: Cherry Lake Publishing, 2013.

WEB SITE

Makey Makey Quick Start Guide
http://makeymakey.com/howto.php
Check out some cool activities on the official Makey Makey Web site.

Sparkfun: Makey Makey Advanced Guide
https://learn.sparkfun.com/tutorials/makey-makey-advanced-guide
Learn more about advanced Makey Makey projects with this helpful guide.

Index

About the Author

A Michigan native, Sandy Ng has fond childhood memories of tinkering and building things with her dad in their garage. Her love for experimenting and creativity stayed with her, leading to a degree in cellular biology while dabbling with design on the side. Sandy earned her MSI in Human-Computer Interaction from the University of Michigan.